D1272171

A Century of Fiction by American Negroes

1853–1952

A Descriptive Bibliography

by

MAXWELL WHITEMAN

ALBERT SAIFER
PHILADELPHIA 1968

Library of Congress Catalog Card Number: 55-10876

INTRODUCTION

The growing interest in literature by Negroes often raises the question, who are the Negro authors and what have they written? This is especially true of the short story writer and novelist. Today the general public is quite familiar with the names of Richard Wright, Frank Yerby and Willard Motley and even a little surprised to learn, by way of the dust jacket blurb, that the latter two best selling novelists writing about non-Negro themes are Negro authors. But this individual popularity sheds no light on those who have been lost in the maze of fiction publishing. In the past quarter century at least a half-dozen books have been published dealing with the Negro as author and character. These efforts have been in the critical field and bibliography has only functioned as an adjunct. One of the first of these books, a slim volume by Nick Aaron Ford, *The Contemporary Negro Novel*, covered the period between 1924 and 1934. In it Dr. Ford stated, "From 1914 to 1924 not a single Negro novel was written; yet during the next ten years, ending with 1934, twenty were produced by a new crop of authors . . ." Actually over sixty volumes of fiction, novels and short stories, were published during the two decades to which Dr. Ford has reference.

The critical examination of the Negro in American literature, such as the excellent study by Sterling Brown, *The Negro in Fiction*, (Bronze Booklet Series No. 6) deals more with the Negro as a character in fiction than as an author so that the Negro author's contribution cannot be measured separately within the field of American fiction. In the field of American bibliography the inclusion of Negro authors has been limited according to their distinction. Note for example Charles W. Chesnutt and Paul Lawrence Dunbar in Merle Johnson's *American First Editions*, the standard guide for collecting first editions in American literature. The inclusion of Chesnutt and Dunbar has been purely on their pioneer efforts and any collector of American literature will know at once the necessity of adding these two writers to their collection. Individual studies of Dunbar and Chesnutt exist to give the student a picture of their work and times. There remains one recent study which warrants attention; Hugh M. Gloster's, *Negro Voices in American Fiction*, (1948) includes a bibliography which is the largest thus far but covers less than half the area.

The purpose of this bibliography is twofold. First, to offer as complete as possible a record of fiction by American Negroes; second, to provide a guide for teachers and students of American literature.

Every venture in bibliography aims at completeness. Yet the field of American Negro literature, because it is vast and investigation of it so recent, provides us with a territory still incompletely explored. It is, therefore, not impossible for future investigators to supplement this body of American literature with new discoveries. What has been true in other fields of book collecting is especially true of the efforts of Negro book collectors, whose discoveries and contributions have made the task of this bibliography an easier one.

The period here surveyed attempts to cover the first century of fiction by American Negroes; from William Wells Brown in 1853 to the end of 1952. The earliest known novel, Brown's *Clotel*, deserves special comment in addition to the textual description. The book appeared in three editions, with three different publishers and under entirely different circumstances. When the English edition appeared in 1853, Brown was known as an anti-slavery writer. Contrary to the customary procedure, the English publisher made no arrangement to distribute an American edition, so that it did not appear until 1864, eleven years later, at the height of the American Civil War. Examined against the background of the war and the popular reading interests of the day, the propaganda value of the novel can be seen in true focus.

At the time of the appearance of *Clotel*, the Beadle Dime Novels Series had become a popular form of literature and flourished with a good deal of success. In 1861, that firm published *Maum Guineas Children*, by Mrs. M. Victor and its anti-slavery content found considerable favor among Union soldiers. Thereafter exciting tales of adventure poured forth from the Beadle presses at a rapid rate. The civilian population looked forward to each new publication with eagerness and, while the North was busy combatting disunion, the dime novel emerged as the chief literature of the Union Army. With such a ready market other publishers arose in an effort to duplicate the Beadle success. The Boston publisher James Redpath, himself an abolitionist, imitated Beadle in price, format and style, but his imitations were in technical composition alone. Beadle's Indian tales were beyond Redpath's province; instead, his dime novels contained as No. 1, Louisa May Alcott's second book, *Hospital Sketches* and the best of European literature was represented by Jonathan Swift, Victor Hugo and Honoré de Balzac. It was in this distinguished company that the first novel by an American Negro was introduced. *Clotelle*, the name now with a new spelling, was No. 2 in the Redpath Camp Fire Series. In literary selection Redpath exceeded Beadle, but he also went a step further in order to project his abolitionist interest. In a footnote at the end of *Clotelle* he expressed the wish that if the little book could help stir the hearts of fighting men to "promote the universal emancipation" its purpose would be served. It is regrettable that no records survive that would indicate the extent of the sale and width of distribution of the paper backed books whose poor physical construction did not provide them with the hardiness to win the battle against time and the elements. The second American edition of *Clotelle* was issued in a more durable dress and may be described as a regular trade edition. Bound in cloth and published by the then well known Boston firm of Lee and Shepard in 1867 it harbored well for the first Negro novel in America.

The second novel by an American Negro had a quiet appearance in London in 1857 and has since been forgotten. *The Garies and Their Friends* by Frank J. Webb, came out under the imprint of a well known British publisher, Routledge of London, who distributed it but did not reprint it in the United States. Perhaps the failure in issuing an American edition contributed to this neglect, but many other American books of the 1850's have also fallen into oblivion. The precedence established by Brown and Webb in having their first creative writing issued at the hands of established publishing firms was unfortunately not perpetuated.

The first short story by an American Negro has been accredited to Frances Ellen Watkins Harper, *The Two Offers*, published serially in three successive issues of *The Anglo-African* for 1859. The little known historical tale, *The Heroic Slave*, by Frederick Douglass which appeared in Julia Griffiths *Autographs for Freedom* in 1853 actually holds historical precedence. If copies of the *Demosthenian Shield* are ever located, more evidence will be made available for the study of the beginnings of fiction by American Negroes. This journal made its appearance in Philadelphia, June 29, 1841 and was edited and published exclusively by a young Negro literary group.* While these items are not part of the scheme of the bibliography the importance they claim as pioneer efforts is too great to be overlooked.

Chesnutt and Dunbar were the first two writers who met with some popular reception whose works carried the imprint of the older publishing firms. But again it can be noted that the pattern of acceptance by regular publishing houses was inconsistent and to this day remains checkered. Since the early 1920's an increasing number of works by Negroes have carried the imprint of prominent publishers and this was a partial outcome of the so named Negro renaissance. This acceptance is an important phase in the development of Negro writing in America and the appended chronology will aid the reader to distinguish at a glance a regular, or established firm, either in its day or at the present time. These will be designated by the letter "R". Smaller publishers, privately printed works or subsidized publications, along with publishers no longer in existence, will be indicated by the letter "P". Books published by Negro firms will be marked "N". The chronology, it is hoped, will give the user a smooth year by year record of the publishing of Negro fiction. In this manner it can be studied from its sparse beginnings to its present status.

It has not been the intention to place special emphasis on first editions, nor to follow the regimen of pure bibliography. This has, however, been done wherever interesting information has come to light, and it has been possible to examine the book in

* Sketches of the Higher Classes of Colored Society in Philadelphia. By a Southerner. Philadelphia, 1841. The author was George W. Williams, a Negro.

order to help determine the original edition of a work. Information in brackets [. . . .] indicates that such material is not found on the title page. The number of pages is mentioned to indicate the length of the book. Complete collations have not been attempted. Publishers advance copies for preliminary and review purposes have been mentioned whenever found. Reprints have been excluded except where they differ textually, change of title, or the addition of an introduction. Variant editions of special significance have been included. All items are books, complete stories in pamphlet or book form with the exception of magazine contributions, which have been excluded, unless the entire issue contained a complete novel. This is the case of two Dunbar novels and Durham's, *Diane, Priestess of Haiti.* In the case of Delaney's, *Blake, or the Huts of America* which appeared serially in *The Anglo-African,* its inclusion was made solely because it is the third known novel by an American Negro. The last exception is *Miralda* by William Wells Brown. It is included in spite of the fact that no copy is known to exist. Some literary historians believe that it is lost in a contemporary periodical, but it is believed to have been published in book form or as a separate as one may judge by the sources indicated. J. Saunders Redding states in *To Make a Poet Black*, page 131, (1939) that *Miralda* appeared in the *Anglo-African* but up to the present time a copy has not been located.

Other bibliographical errors have forced their way into various works and some of those found are here noted: W. Forest Cozart, *The Chosen People*, Boston, 1924; listed as fiction by M. N. Work, *Bibliography of the Negro* and Charles Henry Fowler, *Historical Romance of the American Negro*, Baltimore, 1902, listed by Hugh M. Gloster, *Negro Voices in American Fiction* are omitted. Both of these titles are definitely not works of fiction. In *The New Negro*, edited by Alain Locke, New York, 1925 a novel by Claude McKay, *Color Scheme* is listed. This is actually *Home to Harlem* which was published in 1928; it never appeared under the title *Color Scheme.**

The importance of juvenile fiction has not been overlooked,

* A list of additional titles which have been excluded can be found at the end of the book.

but that field of literature has distinguished itself sufficiently to warrant separate treatment.

Books listed in *The Crisis*, May 1947 as scheduled for forthcoming publication have to this time not been published; for example, Mercedes Gilbert, *You Can Come and Live With Me*, a third novel by William Attaway, and a second novel by Will Thomas did not go beyond the announcement stage. This is indicative of many announcements in the Negro press which infer a greater literary activity than the published record shows.

The steady increase of fiction by Negro authors can be seen in the 1940's, but the banner year is 1953, which goes beyond this study. At least eighteen novels or collections of short stories, chiefly by major publishing houses, were either in the hands of the bookseller or definitely scheduled for publication.

In the preparation of the bibliography Mrs. Dorothy Porter of the Moorland Foundation at Howard University was helpful in supplying information which would not have otherwise been obtained. Miss Jean Blackwell, curator of the Schomburg Collection at the New York Public Library was equally cooperative and W. Edward Farrison of North Carolina College at Durham offered valuable suggestions which have been incorporated. Mr. Barney Chesnick of The Library Company of Philadelphia called my attention to the seldom found copy of the first American edition of Brown's *Clotelle* which has been reprinted in facsimile form through the courtesy of Mr. Edwin Wolf 2nd, the curator.

Bibliographical Section

[ADAMS, ALGER LEROY]

Taffy, a Novel by Philip B. Kaye. [pseud.] New York, Crown Publishers, [1950]. 258 pp.

A presentation of hectic life in Harlem; the main character is at war with society.

ADAMS, CLAYTON. *See* HOLMES, CHARLES HENRY.

AIKEN, A. E.

Exposure of Negro Society and Societies, New York, [No publisher, 1915?]. 31, 1 pp.

Twenty short sketches about life in Harlem.

ANONYMOUS

Confessions of a Negro Preacher. Chicago, The Canterbury Press, 1928. VII, 297 pp.

The plight of a preacher who fails as a writer and at his calling and finally returns to the soil to earn his living as a farmer.

ARTHUR, JOHN. *See* JOSEPH, ARTHUR.

ASHBY, WILLIAM MOBILE

Redder Blood, a Novel. New York, Cosmopolitan Press, 1915. 188 pp.

Intermarriage and *passing*. Liberal white Stanton Birch deserts his wife when he discovers her Negro origin but unable to forget her he finally returns.

ATTAWAY, WILLIAM

Let Me Breathe Thunder. New York, Doubleday, Doran and Company, Inc., 1939. 267 pp.

The depression of the 1930's and migrant labor; Negro characters are secondary.

———, *Blood on the Forge, a Novel.* Garden City, N. Y., Doubleday, Doran & Co., Inc., 1941. 279 pp.

Negroes, whites and immigrant Slavs in the steel industry.

BENJAMIN, R. C. O.

The Defender of Obadiah Cuff.

Title from William J. Simmons, *Men of Mark*, Cleveland, 1887. Further information not available. Not listed in chronology.

BERNARD, RUTH THOMPSON

What's Wrong with Lottery? Boston, Meador Publishing Company, [1943]. 122 pp.

The "numbers" game is attacked from a religious viewpoint.

BLACKSON, LORENZO DOW

The Rise and Progress of the Kingdoms of Light and Darkness; or, the Reigns of Kings Alpha and Abadon. [Illustrated.] Philadelphia, J. Nicholas, Printer, 1867. 299 pp.

The author, who writes that he "has never went to school twelve months in his life" produced purely original folklore full of strange biblical characters. The story is brought up to the time of the Civil War. King Alpha is Christ and Abadon is Satan who fight through the centuries, until at last Abadon is defeated.

BLAIR, JOHN PAUL

Democracy Reborn. New York, Distributed at 1774 Madison Ave., [1946]. 183 pp.

Published January 30, 1947. The narrative of Uncle Skint is a history of slavery in America which is presented in the form of a novel.

BLAND, ALDEN

Behold a Cry. New York, Charles Scribner's, 1947. 229 pp.

Life in the Chicago Negro community during World War I. Social, racial and economic factors are closely interwoven.

BONTEMPS, ARNA WENDELL

Black Thunder. New York, The Macmillan Company, 1936. 298 pp.

An historical novel about the unsuccessful slave insurrection led by Gabriel in Virginia in 1800. Considered the best historical novel of American Negro interest.

———, *Drums at Dusk, a Novel.* New York, The Macmillan Company, 1939. 226 pp.

An historical novel about Haiti and the rise of Toussaint L'Ouverture.

———, *God Sends Sunday.* New York, Harcourt Brace and Company, [1931]. 199 pp.

The adventures of a Negro jockey are colorfully portrayed in Bontemps first novel.

BRAITHWAITE, WILLIAM STANLEY BEAUMONT

The Canadian, a Novel. Boston, Small Maynard & Company, 1901.

Title changed to *Marian Drury.* Information from Braithwaite's typescript in possession of Maxwell Whiteman. Its publication has not been determined in spite of imprint information. Not listed in chronology.

———, *Going Over Tindel, a Novel.* Boston, B. J. Brimmer Co., 1924.

The story of a spiritual experience. Title from Brimmer Trade List of Books for fall 1923. Copy unlocated.

BREWER, JOHN MASON [Editor]

Humorous Folk Tales of the South Carolina Negro. Orangeburg, S. C., The South Carolina Negro Folklore Guild, 1946. XIX, 64 pp.

Humorous and entertaining tales of the South Carolina Negro. The first of a projected series with a foreword by B. A. Botkin.

BRIDGEFORTH, MED

Another Chance, a Novel. New York, Exposition Press, [1951]. 145 pp.

First published in 1927 under the title, *God's Law and Man's*; copy unlocated. A religious story whose moral is to give man another chance for taking God's law and debasing it for man's materialistic gain.

BROCK, EDWARD ELMORE

A Summer Episode.

Mentioned in the Federal Writers' Project publication,

The Negro in Virginia, N. Y. 1942, page 282. Copy unlocated.

Four other novels in manuscript form are said to exist, but no further information about them has been obtained. They are not listed in chronology because of the absence of a date and other pertinent information.

BROCKET, JOSHUA ARTHUR

Zipporah, The Maid of Midian. [Zion, Ill., Zion Printing and Publishing House, c. 1926]. 257 pp.

Based on biblical and Egyptian themes.

BROWN, CHARLOTTE HAWKINS

"Morning," An Appeal to the Heart of the South. [Boston, The Pilgrim Press, c. 1919]. 18pp.

The devotion of a former slave to her master's children.

BROWN, HANDY NEREUS

The Necromancer; or, Voo-Doo Doctor; a Story Based on Facts. [Opelika, Alabama]. Copyright, By H. N. Brown, 1904. 101, 1 pp.

A religious, folkloristic tussle between Mr. Truth and Mr. Lie.

BROWN, LLOYD LOUIS

Iron City. New York, Masses & Mainstream, 1951, 255 pp.

A first novel describing the experiences of a labor organizer and Negro Communist; based on the conviction of an innocent Negro who was arrested while police were seeking the real murderer.

BROWN, WILLIAM WELLS

Clotel; or, the President's Daughter; A Narrative of Slave Life in the United States. London, Partridge and Oakey, 1853. 245 pp.

The earliest known novel by an American Negro. Richmond at the opening of the nineteenth century. Clotel and Althesa are the daughters of Thomas Jefferson's mistress. An intimate knowledge of slavery and the tragic end of Clotel provides a considerable amount of drama.

———, *Clotelle; A Tale of the Southern States.* Boston, James Redpath; New York, H. Dexter, Hamilton & Co., [1864].

104 pp. Cover title reads: Redpath's books for the Camp Fires.

Clotel rewritten for the American publisher and designed in dime-novel format. The character of the president has been altered to that of an American senator. Only two copies located; The Library of Congress and The Library Company of Phildalphia.

———, *Clotelle; or The Colored Heroine, A Tale of the Southern States.* Boston, Lee & Shepard, 1867. 114 pp.

The title of the third edition is again changed but the text is essentially the same as the second edition.

———, *Miralda, or, the Beautiful Quadroon.*

No copy known to exist. Contemporary references only. Mentioned by the Rev. Hollis Read in *The Negro Problem Solved*, New York, 1864, on page 183 following a list of "works" published by Brown. The suggestion here is that *Miralda* is a book rather than a serialized story buried in some obscure journal. Rev. Read spells it as *Miraldo*, but Brown himself gives the title as above in *The Black Man*, first and second editions, New York, 1863. M. N. Work, *Bibliography of the Negro*, gives the publication date as Boston, 1855. Not listed in chronology.

BRUCE, JOHN EDWARD

The Awakening of Hezekiah Jones; a story dealing with some of the problems affecting the political rewards due to the negro. Hopkinsville, Ky. Phila. H. Brown, [1916]. 62 pp.

The title is descriptive of the content. Negro is spelled as given, with a small *n*.

BURGESS, M. L.

Ave Maria. Boston: Press of the Monthly Review, 1895. 33 pp.

Four short sketches of Catholic interest. The author was a nurse.

BURNHAM, FREDERICK RUSSELL

Taking Chances. Los Angeles, Haynes Corporation, 1945. 1945. 293 pp.

Title from A. Spingarn, *Books by Negro Authors* for 1945,

The Crisis, February, 1946. A copy has not been seen for examination.

CALDWELL, LEWIS A. H.

The Policy King. Chicago, Ill., New Vista Publishing House, [1945]. 303 pp.

The "numbers" or policy racket is carefully examined for its social implications.

CHESNUTT, CHARLES WADELL

The Colonel's Dream. New York, Doubleday, Page & Company, 1905. 294 pp.

Chesnutt's last novel is laid in a small southern town after the Civil War. The aristocratic ex-Confederate Colonel French returns south to help rebuild Clarendon. His efforts are in vain. The leading characters are white.

———, *The Conjure Woman*. Cambridge, Printed at the Riverside Press, 1899. 3, 1, 229 pp. A special edition of 150 large paper copies printed for the Rowfant Club of Cleveland, Ohio, prior to the trade edition. Designed by Bruce Rogers.

———, *The Conjure Woman*. Boston, Houghton, Mifflin & Co., 1899. 229 pp.

Seven folk tales; The Goophered Grapevine; Po' Sandy; Mars Jeems Nightmare; The Conjurer's Revenge; Sis' Becky's Pickaninny; The Gray Wolf's Ha'nt; Hot Foot Hannibal. The stories are in dialect and are told by an old Negro gardner, Uncle Julius. Most of the stories appeared in the *Atlantic Monthly*. The first, *The Goophered Grapevine*, in the issue of August, 1887. *The Conjurer's Revenge* first appeared in the *Overland Monthly*.

———, *The Conjure Woman*. [With a Foreword by Joel E. Spingarn.] Boston and New York, Houghton Mifflin Company, [1927]. VII, 229 pp.

Reprinted from the original plates with the title page from the limited edition. Chesnutt in his article for the *Colophon*, Part Five, 1931, *Post-Bellum-Pre-Harlem* described Spingarn's foreword as "flattering", but gives the year 1929 as the reprint date.

———, *The House Behind the Cedars.* Boston and New York, Houghton Mifflin and Company, 1900. 294 pp.

The beautiful heroine, Rena Walden, spends her life in the unhappy atmosphere of *passing.* Thrown between black and white, she learns too late that her only true friend is a black, courageous Negro.

———, *The Marrow of Tradition.* Boston and New York, Houghton, Mifflin and Company, 1901. 329 pp.

Miscegenation, the struggle between a white and octoroon sister, a Negro physician and an anti-Negro riot are the subjects of Chesnutt's second novel. The scene is the south during reconstruction.

———, *The Wife of His Youth and Other Stories of the Color Line*; With Illustrations by Clyde O. DeLand. Boston & New York, Houghton, Mifflin and Company, 1899. 323 pp.

Nine short stories: The Wife of His Youth; Her Virginia Mammy; The Sheriff's Children; A Matter of Principle; Cicely's Dream; The Passing of Grandison; Uncle Wellington's Wives; The Bouquet; The Web of Circumstance. *Passing,* the tragic mulatto theme and prejudice among Negroes.

CHRISTIAN, S. A.

W. H. Councill speaks of a novel written by Mrs. S. A. Christian in his list of books by Negro authors. *See*: *Lamp of Wisdom; or Race History Illuminated.* Nashville, 1898, page 67. No copy has been seen for examination. Not listed in chronology.

CLARK, PETER WELLINGTON

No Badge of Color. New York, 1947.

Title taken from Spingarn list, *Books by Negro Authors* for 1947, *The Crisis,* February, 1948. Mr. Spingarn lists it as an Exposition Press publication, but the publisher disclaims it as their title. It is described as an anthology of creative writing by Negro soldiers of World War II. A copy has not been located for examination. Not listed in chronology.

COLEMAN, ALBERT EVANDER

The Romantic Adventures of Rosy the Octoroon with Some Account of the Persecution of the Southern Negroes during the Reconstruction Period. Boston, Meador Publishing Company, [1929]. 121 pp.

The title is descriptive of the content.

COOPER, ALVIN CARLOS

Stroke of Midnight. [Nashville, Tenn.] By Counterpoise, 1949. XVIII pp.

No. 2 in the Counterpoise series. The story of Judas Iscariot retold.

CORROTHERS, JAMES D.

The Black Cat Club. Negro Humor & Folklore. Illustrated by J. K. Bryans. New York, London, Funk & Wagnalls Company, 1902. 264 pp.

A connected group of folklore tales with a love story. The setting is in Chicago. The author thought poorly of them and regretted their publication.

COTTER, JOSEPH SEAMON

Negro Tales. New York, The Cosmopolitan Press, 1912. 148 pp.

17 Short Stories about the color line and the tragic mulatto with an autobiographical sketch.

CULLEN, COUNTEE

One Way to Heaven. New York and London, Harper & Brothers, 1932, 280 pp.

Cullen's only novel provides a description of Harlem life which differs widely from the exotic portrayals. Sam Lucas, a one armed religious charlatan, is the main character. Church life and the upper class of Harlem supply the background.

———, *My Lives and How I Lost Them.* By Christopher Cat in collaboration with Countee Cullen, with drawings by Robert Reid Maguire. New York and London, Harper & Brothers, [1942]. 160 pp.

Stories and legends about a cat.

DALY, VICTOR

Not Only War. Boston, The Christopher Publishing House, 1932, 106 pp.

The Negro soldier in World War I. The first half of the novel deals with a Negro and a white man in love with the same woman. She is Negro and favors the white southerner. Later the two men meet on a French battlefield. The Negro soldier attempts to rescue the white southerner, but both are killed.

DEAN, CORINNE

Cocoanut Suite; Stories of the West Indies. Boston, Meador Publishing Company, [1944]. 102 pp.

Fourteen short stories about life in Puerto Rico.

DELANY, MARTIN R.

Blake, or, the Huts of America: A Tale of the Mississippi Valley, the Southern United States and Cuba. New York, *The Anglo-African Magazine*, January-July, 1859. Seven installments.

The third American Negro novel was published in a periodical issued by a Negro publisher and editor, Thomas Hamilton. The novel consists of twenty-four chapters and was not completed. A picture of slavery in the southwest slightly imitative of *Uncle Tom's Cabin.*

DEMBY, WILLIAM

Bettlecreek, a Novel. New York, Rinehart & Co., Inc. [1950]. 223 pp.

The first edition appeared under the imprint of A. Mondadari in Milan, Italy, in Italian translation. Bill Trapp is an old white man who lives in seclusion in the heart of a Negro community for fifteen years waiting for something to happen.

DETTER, THOMAS

Nelli Brown or the Jealous Wife, with other sketches, written and published by Thomas Detter, (colored) of Elko, Nevada. This book is perfectly chaste and moral in every particular. San Francisco: Cuddy & Hughes, Printers, 1871. 160 pp.

Sketches of Negro life in Nevada and Idaho, some in dialect. In a one page preface, the author apologizes for his literary deficiency explaining that little education could be had in his native Washington, D. C. Important for its western interest. Copy in the James Weldon Johnson Negro Collection at Yale University.

DICKENS, DOROTHY LEE

Black on the Rainbow. New York, Pageant Press, [1952]. 254 pp.

The main thread of the story is *passing.*

DODSON, OWEN

Boy at the Window, a Novel. New York, Farrar, Straus and Young, Inc. [1951]. 212 pp.

Coin Foreman, a young Negro, is shown in his quest for security and understanding.

DORSEY, JOHN T.

The Lion of Judah. Illustrated by Clovis E. J. Fouché and W. E. Scott. Chicago, Fouché Company, Inc., Publishers. [1924]. 207 pp.

European imperialists attempt to subjugate Ethiopia.

DOWNING, HENRY F.

The American Cavalryman; A Liberian Romance. New York, The Neale Publishing Company, 1917. 306 pp.

The action moves from the United States to Liberia; the theme is miscegenation and its outcome.

DREER, HERMAN

The Immediate Jewel of His Soul; a Romance. St. Louis, Mo., The St. Louis Argus Publishing Co., 1919. 317 pp.

"Story of the earnest Negro trying to rise into great place."

DUBOIS, WILLIAM EDWARD BURGHARDT

Dark Princess, a Romance. New York, Harcourt, Brace and Company, [1928]. 311, [1] pp.

A Hindu princess and an American Negro are the chief characters in this novel which depicts the attempts to organize the darker peoples of the world. It is both satire and fantasy.

———, *The Quest of the Silver Fleece; a Novel.* Illustrated by H. S. DeLay. Chicago, A. C. McClurg & Co., 1911. 434 pp. An advance copy in printed sepia wrapper was issued by the publisher for review purposes.

Cotton is the chief character in DuBois' first novel, which takes place in Toomsville, Alabama. Alwyn and Zora are the two Negroes who quickly distinguish themselves as models of virtue and justice. Zora rises from an uneducated field hand to a teacher in a private Negro school. Southern aristocracy is satirized and northern profits in southern cotton supply the additional economic background. W. S. B. Braithwaite compared it to Frank Norris' trilogy.

DUNBAR, PAUL LAU(W)RENCE

Novels

———, *The Fanatic.* New York, Dodd, Mead & Company, 1900. VI, 312 pp.

Negroes in Ohio during and after the Civil War and the split feelings engendered by the coming of the "contrabands."

———, *The Love of Landry.* New York, Dodd, Mead and Company, 1900. 200 pp.

The journey of a tubercular patient to Colorado. One Negro character of minor importance.

———, *The Sport of the Gods.* New York, Dodd, Mead and Company, 1902. 255 pp. Published in England as, *The Jest of Fate,* London, Jarrold & Sons, 1903. It appeared first in Lippincott's Magazine, LXVII, 515–594, May, 1901, as a complete novel.

The clash of two social systems, the south and metropolitan Harlem in the north, culminates with the psychological destruction of the southern migrants. Two survive and return to re-establish their lives in the south.

———, *The Uncalled.* New York, Dodd, Mead and Company, 1898. 255 pp. Originally appeared in Lippincott's Magazine, LXIV, 579–699, May 1898 with a separate title page.

Dunbar's first novel. An orphan boy accepts the study of the ministry, but his inner spirit forces him to rebel against the bigotry of small town life.

Stories

———, *The Best Short Stories of Paul Laurence Dunbar.* Selected and Edited with an introduction by Benjamin Brawley. New York, Dodd, Mead & Company, 1938. XVII, 258 pp.

Twenty short stories selected from the four collections that follow.

———, *Folks from Dixie.* With illustrations by E. W. Kemble. New York, Dodd, Mead and Company, 1898. 263 pp.

These twelve short stories comprise Dunbar's first collection. Anner 'Lizer's Stumblin' Block; The Ordeal at Mt. Hope; The Colonel's Awakening; The Trial Sermons on Bull-Skin; Jimsella; Mt. Pisgah's Christmas 'Possum; A Family Feud; Aunt Mandy's Investment; The Intervention of Peter; Nelse Hatton's Vengence; At Shaft 11; The Deliberation of Mr. Dunkin.

———, *The Heart of Happy Hollow.* Illustrated by E. W. Kemble. New York, Dodd, Mead and Company, 1904. 309 pp.

Sixteen tales and stories on various phases of post-bellum life. Content: The Scapegoat; One Christmas at Shiloh; The Mission of Mr. Scatters; A Matter of Doctrine; Old Abe's Conversion; The Race Question; A Defender of the Faith; Cahoots; The Promoter; The Wisdom of Silence; The Triumph of Ol' Mis' Pease; The Lynching of Jube Benson; Schwalliger's Philanthropy; The Interference of Patsy Ann; The Homecoming of 'Rastus Smith; The Boy and the Bayonet.

———, *In Old Plantation Days.* Illustrated. Dodd, Mead and Company, 1903. 307 pp.

Benjamin Brawley considered this collection of twenty-five stories the best Dunbar produced.

Content: Aunt Tempe's Triumph; Aunt Tempe's Revenge; The Walls of Jericho; How Brother Parker Fell From Grace; The Trousers; The Last Fiddling of Mordaunt's Jim; A Supper by Proxy; The Trouble About Sophiny; Mr. Groby's Slippery Gift; Ash-Cake Hannah and her Ben; Dizzy-Headed Dick; The Conjuring Contest; Dandy Jim's Conjure Scare; The Memory of Martha; Who Stand for the Gods; A Lady Slipper; A Blessed Deceit; The Brief Cure of Aunt Fanny; The Stanton Coachman; The Easter Wedding; The Finding of Martha; The Defection of Maria Ann Gibbs; A Judgement of Paris; Silent Sam'el; The Way of a Woman.

———, *The Strength of Gideon and Other Stories.* With Illustrations by E. W. Kemble. New York, Dodd, Mead and Company, 1900. 362 pp.

Twenty short stories.

Content: Strength of Gideon; Mammy Peggy's Pride; Viney's Free Papers; The Fruitful Sleeping of the Rev. Elisha Edwards; The Ingrate; The Case of 'Ca'Line; The Finish of Patsy Barnes; One Man's Fortunes; Jim's Probation; Uncle Simon's Sundays Out; Mr. Cornelius Johnson, Office Seeker; An Old Time Christmas; A Mess of Pottage; The Trustfullness of Polly; The Tragedy at Three Forks; The Finding of Zach; Johnsonham Junior; The Faith Cure Man; The Council of State; Silas Jackson.

DURANT, E. ELLIOT AND CUTHBERT M. ROACH

The Princess of Naragpur or a Daughter of Allah. New York, The Grafton Press [1928]. 191 pp.

The Schomburg collection describes the author as a West Indian Negro, but *Who's Who in Colored America*, third edition, lists Durant as an American. An East Indian tale.

DURHAM, JOHN STEPHENS

Diane, Priestess of Haiti. Lippincott's Monthly Magazine LXIX, April, 1902. 387–466.

A Haitian story with German-Haitian business relations

for background. Published with a separate title page similar to Dunbar's, *The Uncalled* and *The Sport of the Gods*. It was never republished in book form.

EARLE, VICTORIA [VICTORIA EARLE MATTHEWS]

Aunt Lindy; A Story Founded on Real Life. Illustrated by Mary L. Payne. New York, [Press of J. J. Little & Co.] 1893, 16 pp.

A fire in Fort Valley, Georgia and its after effects. Negro characters.

ELLIS, GEORGE WASHINGTON

The Leopard's Claw. N. Y. International Authors Association, [1917]. 5, 172 pp.

An exciting story of love and adventure from a European castle to the West African Jungle. African social institutions and their influence upon the inner life of natives revolves about the mysterious function of *The Leopard's Claw* at the beginning of the twentieth century.

ELLISON, RALPH

Invisible Man. New York, Random House, [1952]. 439 pp.

From high school graduation in the south, the story moves to the complex life of Harlem. Its pace is feverish and it provides the reader with a different interpretation of Negro life in America. The National Book Award presented it with the fiction prize for 1953.

ENDICOTT, STEPHEN. *See* ROBERTS, WALTER ADOLPHE.

FAUSET, JESSIE REDMOND

The Chinaberry Tree. A Novel of American Life. New York, Frederick A. Stokes Company, 1931. X, 341 pp.

A two page introduction by Zona Gale. The story of Aunt Sal, Laurentine, Melissa and the Chinaberry Tree. "The home life of the Colored American who is not being pressed too hard by the Furies of Prejudice, Ignorance and Economic Injustice."

———, *Comedy American Style.* New York, Frederick A. Stokes Company, 1933. 327 pp.

Olive Cary is as eager to "pass" as Phoebe Grant is to

identify herself with Negroes. Both are near white, middle class and live in Philadelphia.

———, *Plum Bun. A Novel Without a Moral.* New York, Frederick A. Stokes Company, 1929. 379 pp.

The tempest of *passing* and its resultant ambivalence force Angela into a complicated network of emotional upheaval.

———, *There is Confusion.* New York, Boni and Liveright, 1924. 297 pp.

The Negro middle class is as much governed by respectability and tradition as are those who are not Negro. But they have an additional problem, color. The first of four novels dealing with middle class Negroes as a definite part of American life.

FINCH, AMANDA

Back Trail. A Novella of Love in the South. New York, The William-Frederick Press, 1951. 44 pp.

The love of one man for two sisters and the consequences which follow after his secret marriage to the youngest sister.

FISHER, RUDOLPH

The Conjure Man Dies. A Mystery Tale of Dark Harlem. New York, Covici-Friede, [1932]. 316 pp.

First detective novel with all the participants Negro. The scene is in Harlem where the author was a physician.

———, *The Walls of Jericho.* New York and London, Alfred A. Knopf, 1928. 307 pp.

Harlem intimately examined.

FLEMING, SARAH LEE BROWN

Hope's Highway. New York, Neale Publishing Co., 1917. 156 pp.

The praise of accomplished Negroes is the central purpose of the story. Tom Brimley escapes from a chain gang, is educated at Oxford University and returns south to rebuild a Negro college.

FORD, NICK AARON AND H. L. FAGGETT [Editors]

Best Short Stories by Afro-American Writers. (1925–1950) Boston, Meador Publishing Company, [1950]. 307 pp.

Forty modern short stories selected from the Baltimore *Afro-American*, with a foreword by Carl Murphy of the *Afro-American Newspapers.* The first anthology of its nature.

FULLILOVE, MAGGIE SHAW

Who Was Responsible? Cincinnati, Printed for the Author by the Abington Press, 1919. 181 pp.

Copy unlocated.

GARNER, CARLYLE W.

It Wasn't Fair. New York, Fortuny's [1940]. 47 pp.

Two short stories: It Wasn't Fair; The Contemptuous Town Mouse. Adolescent love episodes.

GHOLSON, EDWARD

From Jerusalem to Jericho. Boston, Chapman & Grimes, [1943]. 122 pp.

The story of the Good Samaritan retold by a minister.

GILBERT, MERCEDES

Aunt Sara's Wooden God. Boston, The Christopher Publishing House, [1938]. 271 pp.

Miscegenation; the conflict between two half-brothers, sons of a white and a Negro father.

GILMORE, F. GRANT

"*The Problem*", *a Military Novel.* [Rochester, N. Y. Press of Henry Conolly Co., 1915.] 99 pp.

William Henderson, a Negro sergeant in the Spanish-American War, is the outstanding character. Near white Freda hesitates to marry him, but sets aside any qualms when she is assured of her Negro origin. Three poems are appended to the novel.

GRAHAM, KATHERINE CAMPBELL

Under the Cottonwood. A Saga of Negro Life in which the History, Traditions and Folklore of the Negro of the Last

Century are vividly Portrayed. New York, Wendell Malliet and Company, 1941. 262 pp.

Five Generations of the Stearns family in Texas.

GRANT, JOHN WESLEY

Out of the Darkness, or Diabolism and Destiny. Nashville, Tenn., National Baptist Publishing Board, 1909. 316 pp.

The main characters are Negroes; a doctor, lawyer and minister. By showing their attainments, they are presented as a bulwark against prejudice and oppression. The doctor is lynched when he falls in love with a white patient whose life he has saved. The lawyer and minister fall into a pattern of complacency.

GRAY, WADE S.

Her Last Performance. Omaha, Rapid Printing & Publishing Co., 1944. 140 pp.

A novel about love and marriage with the main character a pianist.

GRIGGS, SUTTON ELBERT

The Hindered Hand; or, the Reign of the Repressionist. Nashville, Tenn., The Orion Publishing Company, 1905. 305 pp. Three editions appeared in 1905. The third, revised, contains an additional essay on Thomas Dixon: *A Hindering Hand, Supplementary to the Hindered Hand. A Review of the Anti-Negro Crusade of Mr. Thomas Dixon, Jr.* It was enlarged to 333 pp.

An undisguised, unrestrained attack upon Dixon's *The Leopard's Spots* and kindred literature which worked hard to prove that the main object of the Negro was to possess white women. Griggs was more widely read in his time than his distinguished contemporary Dunbar. Today he is hardly known. Griggs was his own publisher and bookseller.

———, *Imperium in Imperio.* Cincinnati, Ohio, The Editor Pub. Co., 1899. 265 pp.

Grigg's first novel is also the first Negro novel of political interest. The author develops the idea of a national Negro organization, Imperium in Imperio. A scheme to acquire the state of Texas as a Negro republic does not meet with success.

———, *Overshadowed.* Nashville, Tenn., The Orion Publishing Company, 1901. 219 pp.

A former Virginia governor is exposed for his extra-marital Negro relations. Disaster overtakes the governor when he is exposed but the Negro is lynched. Negro trade unionists are introduced in the scheme of the novel.

———, *Pointing the Way.* Nashville, Tenn., The Orion Publishing Company, 1908. 233 pp.

Miscegenation, intra-Negro prejudice and politics. A program of cooperation is suggested to improve life in the south.

———, *Unfettered.* A Novel. Nashville, Tenn., The Orion Publishing Company, 1902. 276 pp.

The author, in a setting of conflict and tragedy, attempts to unfetter the mind of the Negro from the burdens imposed upon him. A proposal to improve Negro-white relations is presented in the sequel, "*Dorlan's Plan.*"

GROSS, WERTER L.

The Golden Recovery revealing a streamlined cooperative Economic System compiled from the best authorities of the World, both ancient and modern. [Copyright 1946 by the Golden Recovery Corporation, Reno, Nevada]. 186 pp.

A modern utopia.

HARPER, FRANCES ELLEN WATKINS

Iola Leroy, or Shadows Uplifted. Philadelphia, Garrigues Brothers, 1892, 282 pp.

Contains a three page introduction by William Still, the Philadelphia Underground Railroad agent. Deals with the Civil War and after; slavery and the color line. The first novel by an American Negro woman appeared in three editions, the second and third bearing the Boston imprint of James H. Earle, publisher of books by Negroes.

HARRIS, M. VIRGINIA

Weddin' Trimmin's. New York, The Exposition Press, [1949]. 233 pp.

The mulatto theme and the distress which is avoided by meeting the problem face to face.

HENDERSON, GEORGE WYLIE

Ollie Miss, a Novel. Blocks by Lowell Leroy Balcolm. New York, Frederick A. Stokes Company, 1935. 276 pp.

Life among Negro sharecroppers in Alabama is presented for the first time. Ollie Miss, the heroine is a picturesque figure, strong, beautiful and enigmatic.

——, *Jule.* New York, Creative Age Press, Inc., [1946]. 234 pp.

Jule is the son of Ollie Miss, title of Henderson's first novel. Jule leaves his girl friend, Berta Mae and white friend Rollo for life in Harlem. Title changed to *Jule: Alabama Boy in Harlem.* New York, Avon Publications, No. 577.

HENRY, THOMAS MILLARD

Spring in Virginia.

Title from Work, *Negro Year Book.* Also mentioned in *Who's Who in Colored America* 1930–31–32 (Third Edition). Henry was a professional reader of his own poems and stories in New York. No copy located. Not listed in chronology.

HENRY, WILLIAM S.

Out of Wedlock. Boston, R. G. Badger, [1931]. 220 pp.

Mary Tanner's five illegitimate children by a white common law husband provides the background for a woman who dedicates herself to fighting the circumstances which make possible such a situation.

HILL, JOHN H.

Princess Malah. Washington, D. C., The Associated Publishers, Inc. [1933]. VII, 330 pp.

A pleasant picture of the life of a Negro-Indian slave in colonial America.

HIMES, CHESTER

Cast the First Stone. New York, Coward-McCann, 1952. 346 pp.

The mind of a prisoner after two decades of incarceration.

———, *If He Hollers Let Him Go.* Garden City, New York, Doubleday & Company, Inc., 1945. 249 pp.

An embittered shipyard foreman contends with the prejudice of his white, southern fellow workers during World War II, lashing out violently at the countless humiliations he is forced to endure.

———, *Lonely Crusade.* New York, Alfred A. Knopf, 1947. 398 pp.

Lee Gordon, the main character, is the first Negro Union organizer in Los Angeles. The whole gamut of Negro-white relations are seen through his eyes.

[HOLMES, CHARLES HENRY]

Ethiopia, the Land of Promise; a book with a purpose. By Clayton Adams [pseud.] N. Y. The Cosmopolitan Press, 1917. 129 pp.

An attempt to expose the conditions of abuse, oppression and lynching in the country of "Unionland."

HOPKINS, PAULINE ELIZABETH

Contending forces; A Romance illustrative of Negro life, North and South. With illustrations and cover design by R. Emmett Owen. Boston, Colored Co-Operative Publishing Company, 1900. 402 pp.

In this portrayal of cruelty and injustice committed against the Negro, the author observes in an introductory note about the writing of fiction: "No one will do this for us; we must ourselves develop the men and women who will faithfully portray the inmost thoughts and feelings of the Negro with all the fire and romance which lie dormant in our history, and, as yet, unrecognized by writers of the Anglo-Saxon race."

Another novel, *Of one Blood; or, The Hidden Self* appeared in 12 installments in *The Colored American Magazine*, beginning November, 1902.

HOWARD, JAMES H. W.

Bond and Free; a True tale of slave times. Harrisburg, [Pa.] Edwin K. Myers, 1886. 220 pp. The first edition has a frontispiece portrait of the author omitted from later editions.

HUFFMAN, EUGENE HENRY

"*Now I Am Civilized*". Illustrated by Herbert Rasche. Los Angeles, California, Wetzel Publishing Co., Inc., 1930. 208 pp.

"The satirical reverie of an alert, close observing, and almost entirely illiterate young Negro cook, who, after years of domestic service in the homes of the 'cultured' has commanded a parrot-like fluency of English . . . but barely knows how to write his name."

HUGHES, LANGSTON

Laughing to Keep from Crying. New York, Henry Holt and Company, [1952]. 206 pp.

Interrelated stories on many phases of Negro life from the "twenties" to the present.

———, *Not Without Laughter.* New York, Alfred A. Knopf, 1930. 324 pp.

Negro life in a small non-southern town. Aunt Hager, her three daughters and Sandy, a grandson, are the main characters. The portrayal of Sandy's early years constitutes the main portion of the book. One of the outstanding Negro novels of the 1930's.

———, *Simple Speaks His Mind.* New York, Simon & Schuster, [1950]. 231, [1] pp.

These connected sketches originally appeared in *The Chicago Defender.* They reflect the pathos and humor in the every-day life of the ordinary northern urban Negro.

———, *The Ways of White Folks.* New York, Alfred A. Knopf, 1934. 248 pp.

Fourteen stories dealing mainly with prejudice. The white man is satirized.

HUNTER, H.L.

The Miracles of the Red Altar Cloth. New York, Exposition Press, 1949. 213 pp.

An Italian boy rediscovers his childhood sweetheart when she is engaged to marry her own brother. Title from *Negro Year Book,* 1952.

HURSTON, ZORA NEALE

Jonah's Gourd Vine. With an introduction by Fanny Hurst. Philadelphia, J. B. Lippincott Company, 1934. 316 pp.

Negro folklore and symbolism of the deep south. The checkered story of John, an Alabama Negro, whose fascination for women creates a situation of humor and pathos, joy and heartache. Rich in dialect. Recommended by the Book of the Month Club for 1934.

———, *Moses, Man of the Mountain.* Philadelphia, J. B. Lippincott Company, [1939]. 351 pp.

The biblical Moses recreated and retold from birth to the promised land.

———, *Mules and Men.* With an introduction by Franz Boas. 10 illustrations by Miguel Covarrubias. Philadelphia, J. B. Lippincott Company, 1935. 342 [1] pp.

A collection of Negro folktales chiefly from Florida. Contains a section on Hoodoo.

———, *Seraph on the Suwanee:* A Novel. New York, Charles Scribner's Sons, 1948. 311 pp.

Arvay and Jim Meserve live in the sawmill country on the banks of the Suwanee River in Florida. An exciting story of life in the citrus belt amid shrimping boats and on river plantations. An advance copy in light blue printed wrapper notes that the actual publication date is October 11.

———, *Their Eyes Were Watching God; A Novel.* Philadelphia, J. B. Lippincott Company, [1937]. 286 pp.

The story of Janie's quest for happiness provides the reader with interesting sketches of Negro characters; Janie's Grandma, Joe Starks, her second husband as Mayor of

Eatonville and Tea Cake who brings fulfillment into Janie's life.

IMBERT, DENNIS I.

The Colored Gentlemen. A Product of Modern Civilization. New Orleans, La. Williams Printing Service, 1931. 86 pp.

The author defends the Negro as a human being and a product of the civilization in which he lives. The book contains a directory supplement of prominent New Orleans Negroes who have achieved success.

JARRETTE, A. Q.

Beneath the Sky, A Novel of Love and Murder among the Poor Whites and Negroes of the Deep South. New York, The Weinberg Book Supply Co., 1949. 151 pp.

The title aptly describes the content. Advertising blurbs advise that it is "the novel publishers fear to publish."

JENKINS, DEADERICK FRANKLIN

It was Not My World. A Story in Black and White that's Different. [Los Angeles, The Author, 1942]. 3, 104 pp. Social and economic life of Negroes in the South. "A novel to end all novels" characterizes the writer's mood.

———, *Letters to My Son.* [Los Angeles, Calif. The Deaderick F. Jenkins Publishing Co., 1947.] IX, 111 pp.

A critical review of modern events presented in a series of letters.

JOHNSON, AMELIA E.

The Hazeley Family. Philadelphia, American Baptist Publication Society, [1894]. 191 pp.

A young girl and her friends shown in the light of pure moral Christian teachings. The author was the wife of a Baptist minister from Baltimore, Rev. Harvey Johnson.

JOHNSON, EDWARD AUGUSTUS

Light Ahead for the Negro. New York, The Grafton Press, [1904]. VI, 132 pp.

A Negro utopian novel; the first of its kind. How the Negro "problem" was solved by the year, 2007.

JOHNSON, FENTON

Tales of Darkest America. Chicago, Ill. *The Favorite Magazine,* [1920]. 34 pp.

Six short, short stories and an autobiographical sketch dealing with education and a literary career. Originally published in Johnson's own journal, *The Favorite Magazine.*

[JOHNSON, JAMES WELDON]

The Auto-biography of an Ex-colored Man. Boston, Sherman, French and Company, 1912. 207 pp.

Introduced by Brander Mathews, this cosmopolitan novel of Negro life appeared anonymously. It is not the story of Johnson's life.

———, *The Auto-biography of an Ex-colored Man.* With an introduction by Carl Van Vechten. New York and London, A. A. Knopf, 1927, XII, 211 pp.

Published under Johnson's name with the new introduction.

JONES, JOSHUA HENRY (JR.)

By Sanction of Law. Boston, B. J. Brimmer Company, 1924. 366 pp.

Miscegenation as an affirmative way to help solve racial problems. The hero fights for the right to marry his white fiancee.

JONES, J. MCHENRY

Hearts of Gold, a Novel. Wheeling, [West Va.] Daily Intelligencer Steam Job Press, 1896. 299 pp.

The reconstruction period provides the time of action. Intermarriage is the important thread which entangles a legacy due Regina, a main character. Negroes are drawn favorably against the background of injustices which engulf their lives.

JONES, YORK

The Climbers; A Story of Sun-Kissed Sweethearts. Chicago, Ill. The Glad Tidings Publishing Company, 1912. 191 pp.

The intellectual progress of four Negro college students and the achievement of their professional goals as physician, college professor and minister.

JORDAN, MOSES

The Meat Man. A Romance of Life, of Love, of Labor. Illustrated with scenes from Wm. S. Scott Studio. Chicago, Judy Publishing Company, [1923]. 96 pp.

World War I and after.

[JOSEPH, ARTHUR]

Dark Metropolis. By John Arthur [pseud.] Boston, Meador Publishing Company, 1936. 154 pp.

A novel of life in New York's Harlem.

KAYE, PHILIP B. *See* ADAMS, ALGER LEROY.

KELLEY, EMMA DUNHAM

Megda. Boston, James H. Earle, 1892. 394 pp.

A superficial novel about young people in a private school and their religious conversion. There is no suggestion of Negro characters.

LARSEN, NELLA [NELLA LARSEN IMES]

Quicksand. New York & London, A. A. Knopf, 1928. 301 pp.

Helga Crane is torn between white and Negro and finds no comfort on either side. W. E. B. DuBois considered this portrayal of the tragic mulatto theme as "the best piece of fiction that Negro America has produced since the heyday of Chesnutt . . ." when reviewing the book in *The Crisis.*

———, *Passing.* New York & London, A. A. Knopf, 1929. 215 pp.

Clare Kendry wants to strip herself from the duality of being neither Negro nor white, but when her Negro origin is discovered by her white husband she commits suicide.

LEE, GEORGE WASHINGTON

River George. New York, The Macauley Company, [1937]. 275 pp.

Portrayal of Negro sharecroppers. Scene is World War I and after.

———, *Beale Street Sundown,* New York, House of Field, Inc., [1942]. 176 pp.

Nine short stories about Beale Street. Beale Street Anyhow; It Happened At An Amateur Show; At Beale Street Treasure Hunt; A Beale Streeter Remembers the War; The First Blues Singer; King of the Rousters; She Made A Preacher Lay His Bible Down; Passing; The Beale Street Blues I'm Singing.

LEE, JOHN M.

Counter Clockwise. New York, Wendell Malliet and Company, 1940. 103 pp.

Liom, a white girl, commits suicide when betrayed by her suitor. Helen, of Negro origin, passes as white but is betrayed by her white husband. She escapes the tragic end of her white friend and returns to the security of her Negro mother.

LISCOMB, HARRY F.

The Prince of Washington Square; An Up-to-the-minute Story. New York, Frederick A. Stokes Company, 1925. IX, 180 pp.

Razor wielding Rastus is a minor Negro character among a group of white bootblacks and newspaper boys of whom Jack rises to fame and fortune in Horatio Alger style.

LUBIN, GILBERT

The Promised Land. Boston, The Christopher Publishing House [1930]. 59 pp.

The author describes his story as a "visionary tale." The vision consisting of an effort to turn Liberia into the "Promised Land" for American Negroes.

LUCAS, CURTIS

Flour is Dusty. Philadelphia, Dorrance & Company, [1943]. 166 pp.

Jim Harrell flees the south only to find discrimination in the north, but in spite of it, he meets with success.

———, *Third Ward, Newark.* Chicago-New York, Ziff-Davis Publishing Company, [1946]. 238 pp.

Life in Newark, New Jersey's Third Ward contains a sociological description of Negroes in a congested northern community.

McClellan, George Marion

Old Greenbottom Inn and Other Stories. [Louisville, Kentucky] George M. McClellan, [1906]. 210 pp.

Five short stories: Old Greenbottom Inn; For Annison's Sake; A Creole from Louisiana; Essie Dortch; The Death of Hanover.

McGirt, James Ephraim

The Triumphs of Ephraim. Philadelphia, [The McGirt Publishing Company], 1907. 131 pp.

Eight short stories. Content: Hail the King and Queen; The Test That Failed; At the Mercy of a Slave; In Love as in War; The Return of Mrs. Steele; El Ria; Lifting the Veil; from the Clutches of the Devil.

McKay, Claude

Banana Bottom. New York, London, Harper and Brothers, 1933. 317 pp.

A Jamaican story. Bita Plant is seduced at the age of twelve. She is sent to England to be educated and returned to Jamaica where she marries her father's drayman and settles down to a quiet life.

———, *Banjo, a Story Without a Plot.* New York & London, Harper and Brothers, 1929. 326 pp.

Banjo is the vagabond hero through whom a picture of Negro life in the French port city of Marseilles is accurately presented.

———, *Gingertown.* New York & London, Harper & Brothers, [1932]. [10], 274 pp.

Twelve short stories; six of which take place in Harlem, Content: Brownskin Blues; The Prince of Porto Rico; Mattie and her Sweetman; Near-White; Highball; Truant; The Agricultural Show; Crazy Mary; When I Pounded the Pavement; The Strange Burial of Sue; Nigger Lover; Little Sheik.

———, *Home to Harlem.* New York & London, Harper & Brothers, 1928. 340 pp.

McKay's first novel painted Harlem life in bright colors.

Harlem Glory, an unfinished novel, similar in content, was on exhibition at the Schomburg Collection in the Spring of 1952. *Romance in Marseilles*, reminiscent of *Banjo*, also exists in manuscript form.

MICHEAUX, OSCAR

The Case of Mrs. Wingate. New York, Book Supply Company, 1944. 518, [1] pp.

Nazi activity among American Negroes during World War II. Lurid and sensational. A basic section of the novel is drawn from the author's experience in producing Negro motion pictures. Sidney Wyeth is the autobiographical character.

———, *The Conquest; The Story of a Negro Pioneer, by the Pioneer.* [Anon.] Lincoln, Nebr., The Woodruff Press, 1913., 311 pp.

Micheaux's first novel is a departure from previous Negro novels. It is the story of a Negro pioneer in the Northwest based on the author's own experience.

———, *The Forged Note; a Romance of the Darker Races.* Illustrated by C. W. Heller. Lincoln, Nebraska, Western Book Supply Company, 1915. 15, 521 pp.

Autobiographical. Sidney Wyeth, novelist, travels through the south to sell his book, *The Tempest* (actually, *The Conquest*) to prospective Negro readers. Much criticism of Negro life in the south.

———, *The Homesteader, A Novel.* Illustrated by W. M. Farrow. Sioux City, Iowa, Western Book Supply Company, [1917]. 533 pp.

The life of Jean Baptiste, a Negro farmer in South Dakota and his white girl friend, Agnes, whom he refuses to marry. Instead he marries Orlean, the daughter of a Negro minister and the marriage ends in tragedy and death. Baptiste later marries Agnes when it is learned that she is of Negro origin.

———, *The Masquerade, an Historical Novel.* New York, Book Supply Company, [1947]. 401 pp.

The author acknowledges his indebtedness for the theme

of the novel to Charles W. Chesnutt. It covers the period from the Dred Scott decision to 1870 and the chief character is the Quadroon, Rena. Rena is also the main character in Chesnutt's *The House Behind the Cedars.*

———, *The Story of Dorothy Canfield based on a great insurance swindle — and a woman!* New York, Book Supply Company, 1946. 416 pp.

From Memphis to Harlem, back to Memphis again. Rape, murder and sensationalism.

———, *The Wind from Nowhere. On his ranch in the vast wilderness of the great northwest, where he alone was black, dwelt Martin Eden, a young Negro man of conquest. The strangest love story ever told.* New York, Book Supply Company, 1941. [7] 423 pp.

The 1944 edition contains only 385 pages. Reminiscent of both earlier novels; *The Conquest* and *The Homesteader.*

MILLER, E[ZEKIEL] H[ARRY]

The Protestant, [Boston, Christopher Publishing House, c. 1933]. XI, [13], 122 pp.

A dream on board ship of a series of mishaps befalling Protestant ministers.

MOORE, ALICE RUTH. *See* ALICE RUTH NELSON.

MORRIS, EARL J.

The Cop. A Novel. New York, Exposition Press, [1951]. 126 pp.

A first novel dealing with the life of a Negro policeman. The author was the first Negro state trooper in Michigan. The main character, Ben Bowie, was actually the first Los Angeles Negro to die in World War I with which the first part of the novel deals.

MOTLEY, WILLARD

Knock on any Door. New York, D. Appleton-Century Company, Inc., [1947]. 503, [1] pp.

Nick Romano and Emma Schultz reach for the stars but fall into the Chicago gutter. A novel of American but not Negro life.

———, *We Fished All Night.* New York, Appleton-Century-Crofts, Inc., [1951]. 560 pp.

The Chicago underworld in post-war America. Not of Negro interest.

NASH, T[HEODORE] E[DWARD] D[ELAFAYETTE]

Love and Vengeance; or, Little Viola's Victory, a story of love and romance in the south; also society and its effects. [Portsmouth, Va., The Author, 1903]. 171 pp.

Copy in Springarn Collection, Howard University Library.

NELSON, ALICE RUTH [MOORE] DUNBAR

The Goodness of St. Rocque, and other Stories. New York, Dodd, Mead and Company, 1899. 224 pp.

Fourteen short stories in a New Orleans setting; St. Rocque Chapel, Bayou St. John and carnival customs provide the background.

———, *Violets and Other Tales.* [N. P. Copyright 1895 by the *Monthly Review.*] 176 pp.

Three page introduction by Sylvanie F. Williams. Seventeen tales and sketches and twelve poems, issued under her maiden name Alice Ruth Moore. Work incorrectly gives *Boston Monthly Review*, 1898 for imprint information. Copy located in the Schomburg Collection, New York Public Library.

NELSON, ANNIE [GREENE]

After the Storm, a Novel. Columbia, S. C., Hampton Publishing Company, 1942. 131 pp.

The social implications of a minister's pre-marital relations.

———, *The Dawn Appears, A Novel.* Columbia, S. C., Hampton Publishing Company, 1944. 4, 1, 135 pp.

The cooperative relationship between "Negro workers and their landlords" on a South Carolina plantation.

OFFORD, CHARLES RUTHAVEN

The White Face. New York, Robert McBride & Company, 1943. 317 pp.

From life as sharecroppers in Georgia to dwellers in Harlem.

PAYNTER, JOHN H.

Fugitives of the Pearl. Washington, D. C., The Associated Publishers, Inc., 1930. XI, 209 pp.

Historical fiction. The escape of slaves from Washington in the 1840's is betrayed by a free Negro.

PATTON, LEW

Did Adam Sin? and other stories of Negro Life in Comedy-drama and Sketches. Los Angeles, 1937. 132 pp.

A copy has not been seen for examination.

PETRY, ANN

Country Place. Boston, Houghton, Mifflin Company, 1947. 266 pp.

The personal lives of New England Negroes after World War II.

———, *The Street.* Boston, Houghton, Mifflin Company, [1946]. 436 pp.

A Houghton-Mifflin Literary Fellowship Award. Lutie Johnson lives amid Harlem's squalor and decay. In spite of her efforts to live decently, she falls victim to the unpleasant circumstances of her environment.

PICKENS, WILLIAM

American Aesop, Negro and Other Humor. Boston, The Jordan & Moore Press, 1926. XX, 183 pp.

Contains an introduction by the author on "Humor and Speech." Humorous stories about Negroes.

———, *The Vengence of the Gods, and Three Other Stories of Real American Color Line Life.* Introduction by Bishop John Hurst. Philadelphia, A. M. E. Book Concern, [1922]. 125 pp.

Content: The Vengeance of the Gods; Blood or Opportunity; The Superior Race; Passing the Buck; Tit for Tat; How Colored Soldiers Defeated the Real Enemy of Grand Villars.

PITTS, GERTRUDE

Tragedies of Life. Takes place in the United States. Newark, N. J. [The Author], 1939. 62 pp.

Written for scenario purposes.

POWELL, ADAM CLAYTON [SR.]

Picketing Hell, a Fictitious Narrative. New York, Wendell Malliet & Company, 1942. 254 pp.

A Baptist minister attacks the church and clergy through the medium of the novel.

PRYOR, GEORGE LANGHORNE

Neither Bond Nor Free. (*A Plea*). New York, J. S. Ogilvie Publishing Company, 1902. 239 pp.

The author endeavors to portray dark skinned Negroes favorably.

PURVIS, T. T.

Hagar; The Singing Maiden, with other stories and rhymes. Philadelphia, Walton & Co., 1881. 288 pp.

Short stories, sketches and poems by a Philadelphia author.

RASMUSSEN, E. MICHAEL

The First Night. New York, Wendell Malliet and Company, 1947. 278 pp.

A psychotic Russian and the descendent of an African prince create the background for interracial conflict in St. Thomas, W. I.

REDDING, J. SAUNDERS

Stranger and Alone. New York, Harcourt Brace and Company, 1950. 308 pp.

Negro education in Louisiana before and during World War II.

ROACH, THOMAS E.

Victor. Boston, Meador Publishing Company, 1943. 143 pp.

———, *Samson.* Boston, Meador Publishing Company, [1952]. 239 pp.

Samson Shylock is the hero who introduces a secret

weapon that brings war to an end and inaugurates an international police force.

ROBERTS, WALTER ADOLPHE

Brave Mardi Gras. A New Orleans Novel of the '60's. Indianapolis, Bobbs-Merrill Company, [1946]. 318 pp.

An historical novel which presents New Orleans' Creole aristocracy and their participation in the Confederacy. The author is a Negro of West Indian origin and is so designated at the Schomburg collection of the New York Public Library and the Spingarn collection at Howard University.

———, *Creole Dusk, a New Orleans Novel of the '80s'.* Indianapolis, Bobbs-Merrill Company, [1948]. 325 pp.

The title describes the subject matter.

———, *The Haunting Hand.* Frontispiece by George W. Gage. New York, The Macaulay Company, [1926]. 5, 1, 9, 308 pp.

A detective Novel.

———, *Mayor Harding of New York; a Novel.* By Stephen Endicott [Pseud.] New York, Mohawk Press, [1931]. 271 pp.

———, *The Mind Reader.*

A mystery novel.

Title from publishers blurb; a copy has not been located for examination. Not listed in chronology.

———, *The Moralist.* New York, The Mohawk Press, 1931. 300 pp.

A sophisticated novel about novelists and a touch of the Paris of the "twenties".

———, *The Pomegranate.* Indianapolis, The Bobbs-Merrill Company, [1941]. 313 pp.

The mythical Republic of Caribbea is the scene of love and revolution.

———, *Royal Street. A Novel of Old New Orleans.* Indianapolis, The Bobbs-Merrill Company, [1944]. 324 pp.

A romance of Creole life in the 1840's.

———, *The Single Star, a Novel of Cuba in the '90's.* Indianapolis, The Bobbs-Merrill Company, Inc. [1949]. 378 pp.
Cuba's struggle against Spain.

———, *The Top Floor Killer.* London, I. Nicholson and Watson, Limited, 1935. 319 pp.
A mystery novel.

ROGERS, JOEL AUGUSTUS
From "Superman" to Man. [Chicago, M. A. Donohoe & Co., Printers, 1917]. 128 pp.
A fictional dialogue which takes place on a train. It covers much history and sociology.

ROSBROUGH, SADIE MAE
Wasted Travail. New York, Vantage Press, Inc., [1951]. 90 pp.
A Negro girl in quest for happiness is thwarted by oppression and persecution.

ROSS, GEORGE HAMLIN
Beyond the River; a novel. Boston, Meador Publishing Company, 1938. 307 pp.
A New England youth is caught in the War Between the States.

"SANDA". *See* STOWERS, WALTER H.

SANDERS, TOM

"*Her Golden Hour*". Houston, Texas. [The Author]. 1929. 167 pp.
The discovery of oil in Texas leads to dispossessing Negro families on the oil lands to which they had a rightful claim. Interwoven with a love story.

SAVOY, WILLARD
Alien Land. E. P. Dutton & Company, Inc., 1949. 320 pp.
Kern Roberts is faced with all the problems of Negro prejudice. A novel dealing with the 1930's.

SCHUYLER, GEORGE SAMUEL
Black No More. Being an Account of the Strange and Wonder-

ful Workings of Science in the Land of the Free, A. D. 1933 — 1940. New York, The Macaulay Company, [1931]. 250 pp.

A satirical attack on Negroes and whites. A scientific method of turning Negroes white almost leads to the decay of white southern society. Pure whites learn that they are darker than those who have become "Black No More."

———, *Slaves Today. A Story of Liberia*. New York, Brewer, Warren & Putnam, [1931]. 290 pp.

A tale of modern Liberia; the government against the natives, forced labor and open slavery.

SCOTT, ANNE

George Sampson Brite. Boston, The Meador Publishing Company, 1939. 154 pp.

Short stories about a mischievous boy.

SHACKELFORD, OTIS M.

Lillian Simmons; or, the Conflict of Sections; a Story. Illustrated by William Hamilton. Kansas City, Mo., Burton Publishing Company, [1915]. 210 pp.

Interracial strife between migrant and urban Negroes in Chicago which is ultimately settled.

SHAW, O'WENDELL

Greater Need Below. Columbus, Ohio, The Bi-Monthly Negro Book Club, [1936].

A sharp criticism of the conditions of a southern Negro college.

SMITH, WILLIAM GARDNER

Last of the Conquerors. New York, Farrar, Straus and Company, 1948. 262 pp.

A Negro soldier stationed with the American army of occupation is accepted by Germans on an equal basis, but the ban on fraternization quickly alters the situation. World War II.

———, *Anger at Innocence*. New York, Farrar, Straus and Company, [1950]. 300 pp.

The disinherited of Philadelphia's Negro sections. Ted

and Rodina are the main characters whose hopeless situation leads them to murder and suicide.

SPENCER, MARY ETTA

The Resentment. [Philadelphia, A. M. E. Book Concern, 1921]. 216 pp.

An inspirational story. Silas Miller, a penniless Negro boy becomes the "Hog King of the States." Scene is in and about Philadelphia.

[STOWERS, WALTER H.]

Appointed. An American Novel. By "Sanda" [pseud.] Detroit, Detroit Law Printing Company, 1894. 371 pp.

"Sanda" was the pseudonym of Stowers and his collaborator, William H. Anderson. The locale of the first part of the novel is Detroit and then it switches south. The friendship between a white and Negro ends in the lynching of the Negro, John Saunders. One of the first fictional descriptions of a Negro lynching.

SWADOS, FELICE [MRS. RICHARD HOFSTADTER]

House of Fury. New York, Doubleday, Doran & Co., Inc., 1941. 263 pp.

Young women in a penal institution. Segregation of Negro prisoners.

THOMAS, WILL

God is for White Folks. New York, The Creative Age Press, [1947]. 305 pp.

Beau Beauchamp is rejected by his white father because of a domineering anti-Negro aunt; he is despised by darker Negroes, one of whom betrays him to a lynch mob. Beauchamp escapes and returns home to become the master. The story revolves about the intriguing love between Beau and Elisse.

———, *Love Knows No Barriers.* New York, New American Library of World Literature, [1951]. 207 pp.

Reprint of *God is for White Folks* with minor changes and the new title. No. 832 in the Signet Pocketbook series.

THURMAN, WALLACE

The Blacker the Berry. New York, The Macaulay Company, 1929. 262 pp.

The conflict of intra-Negro color prejudice represented through the problem of black Emma Lou. The section dealing with Harlem describes the famous Negro community as sensational and exotic.

———, *Infants of the Spring.* New York, The Macaulay Company, 1932. 284 pp.

A criticism of the Harlem renaissance movement. The bohemianism and debauchery which tainted the rise of the "New Negro" is part of the picture of the 1920's.

THURMAN, WALLACE and A. L. FURMAN

The Interne. New York, The Macaulay Company, [1932]. 252 pp.

Life among internes and nurses in a large hospital. There is no suggestion of Negro or white characters.

TOOMER, JEAN

Cane, With a Foreword by Waldo Frank. New York, Boni and Liveright, 1923. XI, 239 pp.

A collection of stories, sketches and literary miscellanea. Rural Georgia and Washington Negro society comprise the largest portion of the book. Some of the stories appeared originally in *Broom, Double Dealer, Liberator* and *Little Review.*

TRACY, ROBERT ARCHER

The Sword of Nemesis. New York, The Neale Publishing Company, 1919. 327 pp.

The author, a native of Trinidad, B. W. I., practiced medicine in Hawkinsville, Georgia. He drew upon his native island for background for the novel which appears to have been suppressed by the publisher. Information derived from letter inserted in the Schomburg Collection copy.

TURNER, ALLEN PELZER

Oaks of Eden, a Novel. New York, Exposition Press, [1951]. 135 pp.

A story of the gossip and intrigue of small town life and the influence of parents on their children.

TURPIN, WATERS EDWARD

O Canaan; A Novel. New York, Doubleday, Doran and Company, Inc. 1939. 311 pp.

Chicago after World War I and a picture of the migrant Negroes who settled there.

———, *These Low Grounds.* New York, Harper & Brothers, 1937. 344 pp.

Four generations of a Negro family in Maryland's Eastern Shore.

WALKER, THOMAS HAMILTON BEB

Bebbly; or, the Victorious Preacher. Gainesville, Fla., Pepper Publishing and Printing Company, [1910]. 221 pp.

A narrative of the life of a minister.

———, *J. Johnson, or "The Unknown Man"; An Answer to Mr. Thos. Dixon's "Sins of the Fathers."* De Land, Fla., The E. O. Painter Printing Co., [1915]. 192 pp.

Like Sutton Griggs, Walker also glorified the Negro in countering Dixon's writings.

WALROND, ERIC

Tropic Death. New York, Boni & Liveright, 1926. 282, [1], [2] pp.

Ten related sketches of Negro life and death in the author's native West Indies. Content: Drought; Panama Gold; The Yellow One; The Wharf Rats; The Palm Porch; Subjection; The Black Pin; The White Snake; The Vampire Bat; Tropic Death.

WARING, ROBERT LOUIS

As We See It. Washington, D. C., Press of C. F. Sudwarth, 1910. 233 pp.

The real problem of the south is the white "cracker" and the "We", writes Waring, "who see it" are the "educated Negroes, those of cultured families." These are the two sides of southern life the author tries to reveal.

WATERMAN, CHARLES ELMER

Carib Queens. Boston, Bruce Humphries, Inc., 1935. 198 pp.

Defilee, wife of Dessalines, and Marie-Louise, wife of

Christophe take their stand alongside Josephine, the Creole spouse of Napoleon.

WEBB, FRANK J.

The Garies and Their Friends. With an Introductory Preface by Mrs. Harriet B. Stowe, author of *Uncle Tom's Cabin.* London, G. Routledge & Co., 1857. [4] 392 pp.

Up to the present time, the author's Negro origin has been subjected to doubt. This may be ascribed to the following circumstances: the preface called for, on the title page of the first edition, was substituted by a laudatory note by Lord Brougham explaining that Mrs. Stowe's introduction arrived too late for publication. The Stowe introduction appeared in the second issue of the first edition, by the insertion of a cancel sheet, and in it we read, "The author is a coloured young man, born and reared in the city of Philadelphia." A copy of the first edition is in the Schomburg Negro Collection in New York while the second is in the Spingarn Collection at Howard University. The scene of the second Negro novel takes place in Philadelphia prior to the Civil War and concerns itself with race prejudice, violence and miscegenation.

WEST, DOROTHY

The Living Is Easy. Boston, Houghton, Mifflin Company, 1948. 347 pp.

A South Carolina Negro family removes to Boston, but has difficulty in adapting itself because it is forced to compete with established New England Negroes.

WHITE, WALTER

The Fire in the Flint. New York, Alfred A. Knopf, 1924. 300 pp.

Dr. Kenneth Harper returns to his native Georgia to practice medicine. His efforts to help poor Negroes incur local white hatred. His sister is raped and his brother commits suicide after wreaking vengeance upon the white rapists. Dr. Harper is lynched after giving aid to a white patient.

———, *Flight.* New York, Alfred A. Knopf, 1926. 300 pp.

The Negro bourgeoisie, south and north, receives emphasis

in contrast to poor Negroes. Mimi is the main character who successfully but unhappily crosses the color line.

WILLIAMS, CHANCELLOR

The Raven. Philadelphia, Dorrance and Co., [1943]. 562 pp.

Historical fiction based on the life of Edgar Allan Poe. Particularly interesting for its examination of Poe's views on slavery.

———, *Have You Been to the River? A Novel.* New York, Exposition Press, [1952]. 256 pp.

The story of a religious cult leader, a charlatan, and his betrayal of those who reposed their faith in him.

WOOD, LILLIAN E.

"*Let My People Go.*" [Philadelphia, A. M. E. Book Concern, 1922 ?] 132 pp.

Introduction by Bishop Robert E. Jones of the M. E. Church. Mississippi background; lynching and terror. The McCombs move to Chicago where Robert McComb is elected to Congress and promptly introduces anti-lynch legislation which is favorably passed.

WOOD, ODELLA PHELPS

High Ground. New York, The Exposition Press, 1945. 209 pp.

The author writes, "I have tried to do for my people what Pearl S. Buck has done for the Chinese."

WRIGHT, RICHARD

Bright and Morning Star. New York, International Publishers, [1941]. 48 pp.

Originally published in the *New Masses* for the week of May 10, 1939. A story of Negro and white sharecroppers following the pattern of "proletarian fiction" of the 1930's.

———, *Native Son.* New York and London, Harper & Brothers, 1940. 359 pp.

The most articulate expression of the psychological problems which lead to violence and brutality yet to be put into the form of a novel. Bigger Thomas' twisted character forces him to commit murder. Fearing betrayal, he commits another murder but there is no escape from the circumstances which led to the crime; nor is there any final justice when he is brought to trial.

———, *Uncle Tom's Children. Four Novellas.* New York and London, Harper & Brothers, 1938. 317 pp.

Big Boy Leaves Home, the first of the four novellas, appeared in the *New Caravan* for 1936; *Down By the Riverside* is the second and deals with the anti-Negro discrimination during the Mississippi flood of 1927; *Long Black Song* tells of a seduction of a Negro woman by a white salesman; and the last, *Fire and Cloud*, which won the Story Prize Contest (*Story Magazine*, March, 1938) is of political interest. The second edition of *Uncle Tom's Children* includes *Bright and Morning Star*. Some of the stories were serialized in the Communist newspaper, the *Daily Worker*, prior to Wright's renunciation of Communism.

WRIGHT, ZARA

Black and White Tangled Threads. Chicago, The Author, 1920. 360 pp.

Miscegenation in the old south. The story of three cousins of mixed background. Reviewed in the *Chicago Defender* for November 5, 1921. No copy located in either the Schomburg or Spingarn collections. Copy at the Library of Congress.

YERBY, FRANK

Floodtide. New York, The Dial Press, 1950. 342 pp.

Old Natchez in the decade before the Civil War. Love, easy virtue, a Cuban revolution and slaveholding are all colorfully painted.

———, *The Foxes of Harrow.* New York, The Dial Press, 1946. 534 pp.

New Orleans between 1825 and the Civil War. The narrative of a daring gambler ushered in the first of a series of popular novels all of which have become "best sellers"

———, *The Golden Hawk.* New York, The Dial Press, 1948. 312 pp.

The West Indies in the seventeenth century. A romance of the piratical gentry.

———, *Pride's Castle.* New York, The Dial Press, 1949. 383 pp.

The love of a woman pitted against the aggression of a man.

———, *The Saracen Blade.* New York, The Dial Press, 1952. 460 pp.

The intrigue of thirteenth century Italy.

———, *The Vixens.* New York, The Dial Press, 1947. 347 pp.

New Orleans immediately after the Civil War. The scalawag Laird Fournois and his paramour, Denise Lascals, live amid carpetbaggers and klansmen who terrorized Negroes.

———, *A Woman Called Fancy.* New York, The Dial Press, 1951. 309 pp.

Reconstruction period. Scene switches from South Carolina when sharecroppers flee their poverty and go to Georgia where they meet with success and social standing.

YOUNG, KENNETT

Selene.

Title mentioned by W. H. Councill, *Lamp of Wisdom; or Race History Illuminated.* Nashville, 1898. Copy unlocated. Not listed in chronology.

Chronology

1853	Brown, W. W.	*Clotel; or, the President's Daughter; A Narrative of Slave Life in the United States*	R
1857	Webb, F. J.	*The Garies and Their Friends*	R
1859	Delany, M. R.	*Blake, or, the Huts of America; A Tale of the Mississippi Valley, the Southern United States and Cuba*	N
1864	Brown, W. W.	*Clotelle; a Tale of the Southern States*	R
1867	Blackson, L. D.	*The Rise and Progress of the Kingdoms of Light and Darkness; or, the Reigns of Kings Alpha and Abadon*	P
	Brown, W. W.	*Clotelle; or, the Colored Heroine*	R
1871	Detter, T.	*Nellie Brown, or the Jealous Wife*	P
1881	Purvis, T. T.	*The Singing Maiden*	P
1886	Howard, J. H. W.	*Bond and Free; a True Tale of Slave Times*	P
1892	Harper, F. E. W.	*Iola Leroy, or Shadows Uplifted*	P
	Kelly, E. D.	*Megda*	P
1893	Earle, V.	*Aunt Lindy; a Story Founded Upon Real Life*	P
1894	Johnson, A. E.	*The Hazeley Family*	P
	Stowers, W. H.	*Appointed, an American Novel*	P
1895	Burgess, M. L.	*Ave Maria*	P
	Nelson, A. D.	*Violets and Other Tales*	P
1896	Jones, J. McH.	*Hearts of Gold*	P
1898	Dunbar, P. L.	*Folks From Dixie*	R

1898	Dunbar, P. L.	*The Uncalled*	R
1899	Chesnutt, C. W.	*The Conjure Woman (Two Editions)*	R
		The Wife of His Youth and Other Stories of the Color Line	R
	Griggs, S. E.	*Imperium in Imperio*	N
	Nelson, A. D.	*Goodness of St. Rocque and Other Stories*	R
1900	Chesnutt, C. W.	*The House Behind the Cedars*	R
	Dunbar, P. L.	*The Fanatics*	R
		The Love of Landry	R
		The Strength of Gideon	R
	Hopkins, P. E.	*Contending Forces*	N
1901	Chesnutt, C. W.	*The Marrow of Tradition*	R
	Griggs, S. E.	*Overshadowed*	N
1902	Corrothers, J. D.	*The Black Cat Club*	R
	Dunbar, P. L.	*The Sport of the Gods*	R
	Durham, J. S.	*Diane, Priestess of Haiti*	R
	Griggs, S. E.	*Unfettered*	N
	Pryor, G. L.	*Neither Bond Nor Free*	R
1903	Dunbar, P. L.	*The Jest of Fate (English edition of Sport of the Gods)*	R
		In Old Plantation Days	R
	Nash, T. E. D.	*Love and Vengeance*	P
1904	Brown, H. N.	*The Necromancer or Voo-doo Doctor*	N
	Dunbar, P. L.	*The Heart of Happy Hollow*	R
	Johnson, E. A.	*Light Ahead for the Negro*	P

1905	Chesnutt, C. W.	*The Colonel's Dream*	R
	Griggs, S. E.	*The Hindered Hand; or, the Reign of the Repressionist*	N
1906	McClellan, G. M.	*Old Greenbottom Inn and Other Stories*	P
1907	McGirt, J. E.	*The Triumph of Ephraim*	N
1908	Griggs, S. E.	*Pointing The Way*	N
1909	Grant, J. W.	*Out of the Darkness, or Diabolism and Destiny*	P
1910	Walker, T. H. B.	*Bebbly; or the Victorious Preacher*	P
	Waring, R. L.	*As We See It*	P
1911	Dubois, W. E. B.	*The Quest of the Silver Fleece*	R
1912	Cotter, J. S.	*Negro Tales*	P
	Johnson, J. W.	*The Autobiography of an Ex-colored Man*	R
	Jones, Y.	*The Climbers, a Story of Sun-kissed Sweethearts*	P
1913	Micheaux, O.	*The Conquest; the Story of a Negro Pioneer by the Pioneer*	N
1915	Aiken, A. E.	*Exposure of Negro Society and Societies (Date questionable)*	P
	Ashby, W. M.	*Redder Blood*	P
	Gilmore, F. G.	*The Problem, a Military Novel*	P
	Micheaux, O.	*The Forged Note*	N
	Shackelford, O. M.	*Lillian Simmons, or the Conflict of Sections*	P
	Walker, T. H. B.	*J. Johnson, or "The Unknown Man"*	P
1916	Bruce, J. E.	*The Awakening of Hezekiah Jones*	P
1917	Adams, C. (Charles Henry Holmes, pseud.)	*Ethiopia, the Land of Promise; a Book with a Purpose*	P
	Downing, H. F.	*The American Cavalryman*	R

Year	Author	Title	
1917	Ellis, G. W.	*The Leopard's Claw*	P
	Fleming, S. L. B.	*Hope's Highway*	R
	Micheaux, O.	*The Homesteader*	N
	Rogers, J. A.	*From Superman to Man*	P
1919	Brown, C. H.	*"Morning", An Appeal to the Heart of the South*	P
	Dreer, H.	*The Immediate Jewel of His Soul; a Romance*	P
	Fullilove, M. S.	*Who Was Responsible?*	P
	Tracy, R. A.	*The Sword of Nemesis*	R
1920	Johnson, F.	*Tales of Darkest America*	P
	Wright, Z.	*Black and White Tangled Threads*	P
1921	Spencer, M. E.	*The Resentment*	N
1922	Pickens, W.	*The Vengeance of the Gods and Three Other Stories of Real American Color Line Life*	N
	Wood, L. E.	*"Let My People Go"* (*Date questionable*)	N
1923	Jordan, M.	*The Meat Man*	P
	Toomer, J.	*Cane*	R
1924	Braithwaite, W. S. B.	*Going Over Tindel*	P
	Dorsey, J. T.	*The Lion of Judah*	P
	Fauset, J. R.	*There is Confusion*	R
	Jones, J. H.	*By Sanction of Law*	N
	White, W.	*The Fire in the Flint*	R
1925	Liscomb, H. F.	*The Prince of Washington Square*	R
1926	Brocket, J. A.	*Zipporah, the Maid of Midian*	P

1926	Pickens, W.	*American Aesop, Negro and Other Humor*	P
	Roberts, W. A.	*The Haunting Hand*	R
	Walrond, E.	*Tropic Death*	R
	White, W.	*Flight*	R
1927	Chesnutt, C. W.	*The Conjure Woman. Reprint with J. E. Spingarn introduction.*	R
	Johnson, J. W.	*The Autobiography of an Ex-colored Man. Reprint under the author's name and Carl Van Vechten's introduction*	R
	Anonymous	*Confessions of a Negro Preacher*	P
1928	Dubois, W. E. B.	*The Dark Princess*	R
	Durant, E. E.	*The Princess of Naragapur, or a Daughter of Allah*	P
	Fisher, R.	*The Walls of Jericho*	R
	Larsen, N.	*Quicksand*	R
	McKay, C.	*Home to Harlem*	R
1929	Coleman, A. E.	*The Romantic Adventures of Rosy the Octoroon*	P
	Fauset, J. R.	*Plum Bun, a Novel Without a Plot*	R
	Larsen, N.	*Passing*	R
	McKay, C.	*Banjo, a Story without a Plot*	R
	Sanders, T.	*"Her Golden Hour"*	P
	Thurman, W.	*The Blacker the Berry*	R
1930	Huffman, E. H.	*"Now I Am Civilized"*	P
	Hughes, L.	*Not Without Laughter*	R
	Lubin, G.	*The Promised Land*	P
	Paynter, J. H.	*Fugitives of the Pearl*	N

1931	Bontemps, A.	*God Sends Sunday*	R
	Fauset, J. R.	*The Chinaberry Tree*	R
	Henry, W. S.	*Out of Wedlock*	R
	Imbert, D. I.	*The Colored Gentlemen*	P
	Roberts, W. A.	*Mayor Harding of New York*	P
		The Moralist	P
	Schuyler, G.	*Black No More*	R
		Slaves Today, a Story of Liberia	R
1932	Cullen, C.	*One Way to Heaven*	R
	Daly, V.	*Not Only War*	P
	Fisher, R.	*The Conjure Man Dies*	R
	McKay, C.	*Gingertown*	R
	Thurman, W.	*Infants of the Spring*	R
	Thurman, W. & A. L. Furman	*The Interne*	R
1933	Fauset, J. R.	*Comedy American Style*	R
	Hill, J. H.	*Princess Malah*	N
	McKay, C.	*Banana Bottom*	R
	Miller, E. N.	*The Protestant*	P
1934	Hughes, L.	*The Way of White Folks*	R
	Hurston, Z. N.	*Jonah's Gourd Vine*	R
1935	Henderson, G. W.	*Ollie Miss*	R
	Hurston, Z. N.	*Mules and Men*	R

1935	Roberts, W. A.	*The Top Floor Killer*	P
	Waterman, C. E.	*Carib Queens*	P
1936	Bontemps, A.	*Black Thunder*	R
	Joseph, A. (J. Arthur, pseud.)	*Dark Metropolis*	P
	Shaw, O. W.	*Greater Need Below*	N
1937	Hurston, Z. N.	*Their Eyes Were Watching God*	R
	Lee, G. W.	*River George*	R
	Patton, L.	*Did Adam Sin?*	P
	Turpin, W. E.	*These Low Grounds*	R
1938	Dunbar, P. L.	*Best Short Stories. Edited by B. Brawley*	R
	Gilbert, M.	*Aunt Sara's Wooden God*	P
	Ross, G. H.	*Beyond the River*	P
	Wright, R.	*Uncle Tom's Children*	R
1939	Attaway, W.	*Let Me Breathe Thunder*	R
	Bontemps, A.	*Drums at Dusk*	R
	Hurston, Z. N.	*Moses Man of the Mountain*	R
	Pitts, G.	*Tragedies of Life*	P
	Scott, A.	*George Simpson Brite*	P
	Turpin, W. E.	*O Canaan!*	R
1940	Garner, C. W.	*It Wasn't Fair*	P
	Lee, J. M.	*Counter Clockwise*	P
	Wright, R.	*Native Son*	R

1941	Attaway, W.	*Blood on the Forge*	R
	Graham, K. C.	*Under the Cottonwood*	P
	Micheaux, O.	*The Wind from Nowhere*	N
	Roberts, W. A.	*The Pomegranate*	R
	Swados, F.	*House of Fury*	R
	Wright, R.	*Bright and Morning Star*	P
1942	Cullen, C.	*My Lives and How I Lost Them*	R
	Jenkins, D. F.	*It Was Not My World . . .*	P
	Lee, G. W.	*Beale Street Sundown*	P
	Nelson, A. G.	*After the Storm*	P
	Powell, A. C.	*Picketing Hell*	P
1943	Bernard, R. T.	*What's Wrong With Lottery?*	P
	Gholson, E.	*From Jerusalem to Jericho*	P
	Lucas, C.	*Flour is Dusty*	P
	Offord, C. R.	*The White Face*	R
	Roach, T. E.	*Victor*	P
	Williams, C.	*The Raven*	P
1944	Dean, C.	*Cocoanut Suite*	P
	Gray, W. S.	*Her Last Performance*	P
	Micheaux, O.	*The Case of Mrs. Wingate*	N
	Nelson, A. G.	*The Dawn Appears*	P
	Roberts, W. A.	*Royal Street*	R
1945	Caldwell, L. A. H.	*The Policy King*	P

1945	Himes, C.	*If He Hollers Let Him Go*	R
	Wood, O. P.	*High Ground*	P
1946	Brewer, J. M. (Editor)	*Humorous Folk Tales of the South Carolina Negro*	P
	Burnham, F. R.	*Taking Chances*	P
	Gross, W. L.	*The Golden Recovery*	P
	Henderson, G. W.	*Jule*	P
	Lucas, C.	*Third Ward, Newark*	P
	Micheaux, O.	*The Story of Dorothy Canfield*	N
	Petry, A.	*The Street*	R
	Roberts, W. A.	*Brave Mardi Gras*	R
	Yerby, F.	*The Foxes of Harrow*	R
1947	Blair, J. P.	*Democracy Reborn*	P
	Bland, A.	*Behold a Cry*	R
	Himes, C.	*Lonely Crusade*	R
	Jenkins, D. F.	*Letters to My Son*	P
	Micheaux, O.	*The Masquerade*	N
	Motley, W.	*Knock on any Door*	R
	Petry, A.	*Country Place*	R
	Rasmussen, E. M.	*The First Night*	P
	Thomas, W.	*God Is For White Folks*	P
	Yerby, F.	*The Vixens*	R
1948	Hurston, Z. N.	*Seraph on the Suwanee*	R
	Roberts, W. A.	*Creole Dusk*	R

1948	Smith, W. G.	*Last of the Conquerors*	R
	West, D.	*The Living Is Easy*	R
	Yerby, F.	*The Golden Hawk*	R
1949	Cooper, A. C.	*Stroke of Midnight*	P
	Harris, M. V.	*Weddin' Trimin's*	P
	Hunter, H. L.	*The Miracles of the Red Altar Cloth*	P
	Jarrette, A. Q.	*Beneath the Sky*	P
	Roberts, W. A.	*The Single Star*	R
	Savoy, W.	*Alien Land*	R
	Yerby, F.	*Pride's Castle*	R
1950	Demby, W.	*Beetlecreek*	R
	Ford, N. A. & H. L. Faggett (Eds.)	*Best Short Stories by Afro-American Writers (1925–1950)*	P
	Hughes, L.	*Simple Speaks His Mind*	R
	Kaye, P. B. (Pseud.) Adams, Alger Leroy	*Taffy*	R
	Redding, J. S.	*Stranger and Alone*	R
	Smith, W. G.	*Anger at Innocence*	R
	Yerby, F.	*Floodtide*	R
1951	Bridgeforth, M.	*Another Chance*	P
	Brown, L. L.	*Iron City*	P
	Dodson, O.	*Boy at the Window*	R
	Finch, A.	*Back Trail*	P

1951	Morris, E. J.	*The Cop*	P
	Motley, W.	*We Fished All Night*	R
	Rosbrough, S. M.	*Wasted Travail*	P
	Thomas, W.	*Love Knows No Barriers* (*Reprint of God Is For White Folks*)	R
	Turner, A. P.	*Oaks of Eden*	P
	Yerby, F.	*A Woman Called Fancy*	R
1952	Dickens, D. L.	*Black on the Rainbow*	P
	Ellison, R.	*Invisible Man*	R
	Himes, C.	*Cast the First Stone*	R
	Hughes, L.	*Laughing to Keep From Crying*	R
	Roach, T. E.	*Samson*	P
	Williams, C.	*Have You Been to the River?*	P
	Yerby, F.	*The Saracen Blade*	R

Supplement of Fiction by American Negroes for 1953

ARNOLD, ETHEL NISHUA

She knew No Evil. New York, Vantage Press, 1953. 76 pp.
March publication.

BALDWIN, JAMES

Go Tell it on the Mountain. New York, Alfred A. Knopf, 1953. 303 pp.
May publication.

BREWER, J. MASON

The Word of the Brozos: Negro preacher tales from the Brozos Bottoms of Texas. Foreword by J. Frank Dobie. Austin: The University of Texas Press. 1953.

BROOKS, GWENDOLYN

Maud Martha. New York, Harper & Brothers, 1953. 180 pp.

FISHER, WILLIAM

The Waiters. Cleveland and New York, The World Publishing Company, 1953. 295 pp.
February publication.

GROVES, JOHN WESLEY

Pyrrhic Victory, A Collection of Short Stories. Philadelphia, United Publishers, 1953. 60 pp.
January publication.

HOUGH, FLORENZ H.

Black Paradise, a Novel. Philadelphia, Dorrance & Company, 1953. 236 pp.

HUGHES, LANGSTON

Simple Takes a Wife. New York, Simon and Schuster, 1953. 241 pp.
May publication.

KENNEDY, MARK

The Pecking Order. New York, Appleton-Century-Crofts, 1953. 278 pp.

LAMING, GEORGE

In the Castle of My Skin. New York, McGraw-Hill, 1953. XII, 313 pp.

LUCAS, CURTIS

Forbidden Fruit. New York, Universal Publishing, 1953. 135 pp.

PETRY, ANN

The Narrows. Boston, Houghton Mifflin Co., 1953. 428 pp.

August publication.

SMYTHWICK, CHARLES A. (JR.)

False Measure. New York, The William-Frederick Press, 1953.

THOMAS, WILL

The Seeking. New York, A. A. Wyn Inc., 1953. 290 pp

WALKER, MARGARET. [MRS. MARGARET ALEXANDER]

Completing a Civil War novel. Title unannounced at this writing.

WAMBLE, THELMA

All in the Family. New York, New Voices Publishing Company, [1953]. 199 pp.

April publication.

WARD, THOMAS P.

The Right to Live. New York, Pageant Press, 1953.

WRIGHT, RICHARD

The Outsider. New York, Harper & Brothers, 1953. 405 pp.

February publication.

YERBY, FRANK

The Devil's Laughter. New York, The Dial Press, 1953 376 pp.

Excluded Titles

BENNEVILLE, JAMES SEQUIN DE

George Brandt. Boston, The Christopher Publishing House, (1941).

This title is found in several collections of Negro literature but the author is not a Negro.

CUTHBERT, CLIFTON

The Robbed Heart. New York, L. B. Fischer, 1945.

The author is incorrectly listed as a Negro in the *Negro Yearbook* for 1947.

DURHAM, RICHARD

Jet for November 15, 1951 (Volume 1, No. 3, p. 59) speaks of a novel by Durham dealing with a navy riot during World War II. It was scheduled for publication by Julian Messner but no record of its appearance has been found.

FLANAGAN, THOMAS JEFFERSON

The *Negro Review*, Atlanta, Georgia for December, 1953, p. 56 refers to a novel, *Jimson Weeds.* Its publication has not been determined.

GORDON, TAYLOR

Born to Be. New York, Covici-Friede, Publishers, 1929.

Frequently referred to as fiction but the work is actually autobiography.

McGEE, ALICE E.

Black America Abroad. Boston, Meador Publishing Company, 1941.

The author is Negro but the work is not fiction. Listed as fiction in the *Negro Yearbook*, 1947.

STEWART, OLLIE. (Editor)

This is our War. Selected stories of six war correspondents who were sent overseas by Afro-American newspapers.

Journalism not fiction.